SICILY TRAVEL GUIDE 2023

A Comprehensive And Essential Guide To Plan Your Trip To Sicily, Everything You Need To Know

ALICE D. MORALES

Sicily travel guide 2023

Copyright © 2023 by Alice D. Morales

All rights reserved. No part of this publication may be reproduced, distributed, or transmitted in any form or by any means, including photocopying, recording, or other electronic or mechanical methods, without the prior written permission of the publisher, except in the case of brief quotations embodied in critical reviews and certain other noncommercial uses permitted by copyright law. For permission requests, write to the publisher at the address below.

Sicily travel guide 2023

Table Of Contents:

INTRODUCTION TO SICILY..5
CHAPTER 1..8
    Interesting Facts About Sicily...8
    History Of Sicily..19
    Geography And Climate Of Sicily................................22
    Culture Of The Sicilians..25
    The Sicilians And Their Disposition To Visitors.........27
CHAPTER 2..31
    Visa & ID Requirements to visit Sicily.......................31
    Common Italian & Sicilian Phrases You Should Know. 34
    When To Visit Sicily For The Best Experience...........36
    Packing And Equipment Guide To Sicily....................40
CHAPTER 3..43
    Interesting Things To Do In Sicily................................43
    Top Attractions To Visit In Sicily....................................46
    Recommended Hotels To Lodge In Sicily....................77
    Suggested Restaurants To Eat In Sicily........................84
    Cuisines To Try On Your Visit To Sicily........................94
CHAPTER 4..101
    Practical Steps To Avoid Crowd When Touring In Sicily..101
    1-Week itinerary...103
    Festivals You Are Likely To Celebrate On Your Vacation In Sicily..107
CONCLUSION..110

Sicily travel guide 2023

INTRODUCTION TO SICILY

When John finally had the opportunity to travel to Sicily, he was ecstatic since he had always been captivated by the island's culture and history. He was immediately taken aback by Palermo's bustling streets, colorful architecture, and energetic vibe. Yet he didn't appreciate Sicily's enchantment until he traveled beyond the city.

John's visit to the Valley of the Temples in Agrigento was among his most memorable travel moments. He was taken back in time to the days of ancient Greece as he strolled around the historic structures. John was in awe of the magnificent temples and buildings and felt a sense of reverence and amazement as he took them in.

Yet more than simply historical sites contributed to John's journey to Sicily becoming a life-changing experience. He also had the opportunity to sample some of the island's delectable cuisine, which included pasta dishes, fresh seafood, and of course, cannoli. The excellent caliber of the ingredients and the expertise of the regional chefs pleased him, and he enjoyed exploring the neighborhood markets and trying out new foods.

John's visit to Mount Etna was another exciting part of his journey. He was ecstatic to explore the volcano's distinctive landscape as a lover of nature, and he was astounded by the breathtaking views from the peak. Even better, he got to sample some of the region's wine, which was made from grapes cultivated in the rich volcanic soil.

John's trip to Sicily was undoubtedly memorable overall. He adored the island's fascinating past, breathtaking scenery, and delectable cuisine, but most of all, he was moved by the friendliness and warmth of the locals. With a renewed love for Sicilian culture and a strong desire to visit this enchanted island again in the future, he returned home.

Sicily, an independent territory of Italy, is the biggest island in the Mediterranean Sea. The Messina Strait divides it from the Italian Peninsula in the south. The island is renowned for its stunning beaches, rich culture, and history. The island has been shaped by ancient Greeks, Romans, Arabs,

Normans, and Spaniards, and as a result, it is a melting pot of many civilizations.

The city of Palermo, which serves as the island's capital, is a bustling place full of lively markets, quaint cafés, and breathtaking historical sites.

The Palatine Chapel, a masterwork of Arab-Norman architecture with elaborate mosaics and marble sculptures, is the city's most well-known sight.

Sicily is also well-known for its wonderful food, which combines Arabic and Mediterranean tastes. Seafood, spaghetti, and desserts like cannoli and cassata are all staples of the island's native cuisine.

With its undulating hills, luscious vineyards, and aromatic orange orchards, the island's landscape is no less magnificent. The towering volcano Mount Etna, which dominates the island's center, is the most well-known natural feature. The mountain was revered by the ancient Greeks and is said to be the residence of Hephaestus, the deity of fire.

The beaches and coastal towns of Sicily are also well-known. In the cities of Taormina, Cefalu, and Agrigento, you may find some of the most renowned beaches.

Sicily is a friendly, welcoming location where guests are greeted with open arms and treated like family. Sicily is a must-visit location for anybody wishing to experience the finest of Italy, thanks to its rich history, culture, the beauty of the natural world, and delectable cuisine.

CHAPTER 1

Interesting Facts About Sicily

It won't matter whether you visit Sicily for a week or just a few days, spending time in Catania, Palermo, Taormina, or any other lesser-known Sicilian hamlet, you can't help but fall in love with the island.

Sicily, the biggest island in the Mediterranean, is home to many little, colorful communities, stunning beaches, ancient ruins with connections to Greece and Byzantium, as well as mouthwatering cuisine.

The island is the ideal vacation spot for history buffs, foodies, and environment enthusiasts alike, and it is the location of some of the well-known "1 EUR homes" you've heard of.

Here are some intriguing details to consider before making your travel plans to Sicily, which offers many undiscovered treasures to explore.

People from modern-day Lebanon established Palermo.

In 734 B.C., inhabitants of what is now Lebanon, the Phoenicians, established Palermo, the island's capital and one of its earliest towns. Later, Palermo was dominated by the Carthaginians, a Phoenician-related culture from North Africa.

For 1500 years, the majority of Sicily spoke Greek.

Almost 2800 years ago, the first Greek immigrants came. Before the Roman invasion, they ruled the island for 500 years. Nevertheless, during the 700 years of Roman control, the island preserved its Hellenistic culture.

The island was also governed by the Greek-speaking Byzantine Empire for an additional 400 years after the fall of the Roman Empire. Kiri's Zorba almost replaced Don Corleone in our scenario!

Sicily travel guide 2023

Messina was the epicenter of the epidemic.

Apocalyptic events fit for a Hollywood film were about to strike Messina some 700 years before the Covid-19 outbreak.

The first "death-ships" appeared in the area of the city in 1347, with all of the crew and passengers either dead or dying and their corpses covered with revolting buboes leaking pus and blood. It turned out that it was the start of the Black Death, an epidemic that ultimately claimed the lives of between a fourth and a half of the people in Europe. Our Covid-19 dilemma looks like a tiny annoyance in comparison.

Seventeen times, lava submerged Catania.

It has always been dangerous to reside under Mount Etna's shadow, Sicily's most renowned active volcano. In the lengthy history of Catania, lava covered the city 17 times, leaving behind successive layers of archeological evidence. The Roman city, which was constructed on the Greek city, may be found underneath the present-day city. Given the vista, I wouldn't move either!

The biggest city in Greece during the time was Syracuse.

Syracuse expanded to become the biggest Greek city of its day during the tenure of Hiero II, the local monarch. Syracuse, one of the world's largest cities at the time, was a cultural, scientific, and economic powerhouse. One shouldn't be shocked if, in a few centuries, New York or London is little more than quiet backwaters.

One of the world's biggest Islamic cities was Palermo.

When the Islamic Emirate of Sicily was in existence in 1050 A.D., Palermo—then the third-largest city in Europe after Byzantine Constantinople and Islamic Cordoba—became one of the most significant Islamic towns in the world. While Christian Northern Europe was a somewhat savage region, replete with violence, fanaticism, and superstition, under Arabic authority Palermo was a significant center of study, culture, and trade.

Sicily travel guide 2023

Vikings ruled Sicily at one time.

The island was a Norman monarchy for more than 150 years, from 1038 to 1198 A.D. During the first decade of the tenth century, Vikings moved to Normandy and eventually became the Normans. Together, the Normans and Varangian mercenaries—the Swedish counterparts of the Danish and Norwegian Vikings—conquered Sicily from the Arabs. Can you envision Viking spaghetti?

Germany formerly controlled Sicily.

In its history, Sicily has been a component of two different Germanic kingdoms and once was a German kingdom.

The Germanic Vandals first took control of Sicily during the last years of the Roman Empire. They governed the island until the Byzantines wiped them out in 535 A.D.

Then, from 1197 until 1266 A.D., the Hohenstaufens reigned over the Kingdom of Sicily. The future Frederick II Barbarossa of the Holy Roman Empire was King Frederick of Sicily (a medieval Empire based in Germany, not to be confused with the ancient Roman Empire).

Last but not least, the Austrian Habsburg emperors ruled the Kingdom of Sicily between 1720 and 1734.

Spain ruled Sicily at the time.

The island was also a Spanish property for hundreds of years, which may seem unbelievable. First, from 1282 to 1713, Sicily was controlled by members of the Aragonese royal line, first as a sovereign state and then as a province of the Crown of Aragon and afterward the Spanish Crown. After a short period of Savoyard and Austrian Habsburg control, Sicily was once again ruled by Spain under the Bourbon dynasty. When the Kingdom of Italy was founded in 1860, Spanish rule came to an end.

The present rivalry between the two countries in football (also known as soccer) may be explained by this.

Malta spent 700 years as a component of the Kingdom of Sicily.

A free EU exists today. From 1091 until 1814, when it became a British Protectorate, Malta was a part of the Kingdom of Sicily. The Order of Saint John of Jerusalem, often known as the Knights of Malta or Knights Hospitaller, has been in charge of Malta since 1530, even though they were formally a subordinate state of the Kingdom of Sicily.

The first "heat ray" ever utilized by humans was created in Sicily.

As Rome gained control following Hiero's demise, it decided to invade Sicily and put an end to the independence of Syracusa. But they were about to have a shocker!

By use of magical devices created by the renowned local inventor Archimedes, Syracuse was shielded from attack; yet, the vigorous resistance resulted in a lengthy siege. Archimedes is credited with creating a heat ray weapon, which he allegedly used to set Roman ships on fire, among other amazing inventions. Sadly, the city did fall to the Romans in

212 B.C., and a Roman soldier murdered Archimedes despite the proconsul's instructions to spare him.

One of the earliest contemporary vacation spots that welcomed LGBTQ travelers was Taormina.

Taormina rose to prominence as a favored vacation spot for LGBTQ travelers in the latter part of the 19th century. Wilhelm von Gloeden, a German photographer who immigrated to Taormina in 1877, helped the city become one of the progressive leisure hubs of the Western world by luring homosexuals from the oppressive societies of the time. The British Empire was a particularly dangerous place to live for homosexuals, as evidenced by Oscar Wildes' conviction in 1895 and subsequent two-year sentence to hard labor.

The Sicilian Mafia supported the Allies in their fight with the Nazis.

The saying goes, "My adversary is my buddy." During the Allied invasion of Sicily, that was unquestionably true.

Nazi Germany had a sizable military force stationed on the island by 1943. Because of their hatred for Mussolini, the Sicilian Mafia provided information to aid the Allies' amphibious invasion of Sicily, including plans of the island's ports, photos of its coastline, and the names of reliable sources inside the gang.

The best-preserved Classical Greek architecture is found in Sicily.

With the Parthenon in Athens as a close second, the Temple of Concordia in Agrigento is the best-preserved Doric temple in the whole world. However, it's noteworthy to note that not all archaeologists agree that the location was a temple to the goddess Concordia; we'll likely never know to whose deity this site of devotion was devoted. Even so, it looks fantastic!

A valley is NOT what the Valley of the Temples is.

The Valley of the Temples in Agrigento is now one of the top tourist destinations. The greatest collection of these structures outside of mainland

Greece may be found there, which is made up of the remnants of seven Doric-style Greek temples from antiquity. The location is a ridge, not a valley, as you'll undoubtedly realize when you're there.

The British and Americans bombarded Catania 87 times.

Due to its two German airfields, Catania was the target of intense Allied bombing during World War II; it endured 87 bombings, severely destroying several areas of the city and killing some 750 people. On August 5, 1943 (AD), British Forces finally made their way into Catania.

Extraterrestrials were exposed to Sicilian music.

Sicily has a long and very diversified past, and as a result, its traditional music has more roots in Greek, Byzantine, Arabic, and Spanish culture than in Italian culture.

A Sicilian sulfur mine lament was chosen for the Voyager Golden Record by American musicologist Alan Lomax as a result of his study of Sicilian folk music. That depressing Sicilian ballad will be among the first pieces of human music that E.T. will ever hear when the Voyager spacecraft eventually encounters an extraterrestrial civilization.

Sicilians are native speakers of the language.

The majority of Sicily's population now speaks both Sicilian and Italian. With strong Greek, Spanish, Arabic, Catalan, and French influences, Sicilian is a unique Romance language related to Italian. Additionally, the areas of Salento and Calabria speak related dialects. Sicilian is mostly used in informal, familial settings, and the majority of islanders speak a Sicilian-Italian hybrid known as the regional Italian of Sicily.

7 heritage sites that can be found in Sicily.

It put seven sites on the Heritage List due to their fascinating history and stunning natural beauty. As follows:

- Agrigento's Valley of the Temples
- Villa Romana del Casale
- Aeolian Islands
- The Late Baroque Towns of Val di Noto

- Syracuse and the Rocky Necropolis of Pantalica
- Mount Etna
- Arab-Norman Palermo and the Cathedral Churches of Cefalú and Monreale
- The Aeolian Islands Were Reportedly Swallowed by the Sea

The Aeolian Islands were allegedly "swallowed up by the sea" during a period of volcanic activity, according to a myth that surfaced in worldwide publications on January 1st, 1909. The islands were hardly inconvenienced other than a brief interruption in connectivity.

History Of Sicily

Sicily is an island in the Mediterranean Sea that has a long and varied history that dates back to the prehistoric era. Several different cultures and peoples have lived on the island, each of whom has had a distinctive impact on Sicilian history.

Prehistoric Sicily

Sicily's early traces of human occupation date to the

Paleolithic era, or roughly 8000 BC. The Sicani, an island native, and the Sicels, who migrated from the Italian mainland circa 1200 BC, later colonized the island. Throughout the eighth and seventh century BC, Sicily was settled by Phoenicians, Greeks, and Carthaginians.

Roman and Greek Periods

During the fifth and fourth centuries BC, Sicily saw extensive fighting between the Greeks and the Carthaginians. On the island, the Greeks founded several thriving city-states, including Syracuse, which, under the tyrant, Dionysius in the 4th century BC, rose to become the most important city in Sicily. Sicily was taken over by the Roman Republic in 241 BC, and it later developed into a significant grain-producing province.

Medieval Period

Sicily was taken over by the Vandals in the fifth century AD, and then by the Byzantines in the sixth. The Arabs later invaded the island in the ninth century, bringing Islamic culture and architecture with them. Palermo flourished as a significant commercial and cultural hub when under the Arab administration. The Normans conquered Sicily in the eleventh century, where they founded a monarchy that persisted until the twelve. Sicily under Norman's dominion went through a time of cultural and architectural growth, with the creation of well-known structures like the Capella Palatina in Palermo.

Periods of Spanish and the Bourbons

The Kingdom of Sicily was dominated by the Spanish in the fifteenth century, who was later succeeded by the House of Bourbon. Sicily was largely independent at this time, having its own parliament and legal system. Sicily emerged as a hub of Italian nationalism in the 19th century, and the Kingdom of Italy seized it in 1860.

The modern period

Sicily served as a vital theater of conflict between the Allies and the Axis forces during World War Two. The island was brutally bombed, and the Allied invasion of Sicily in July 1943 signaled the start of Italy's deliverance from fascism. Following the war, Sicily went through a period of economic and social development, and in the 1950s and 1960s, it rose to prominence as a major tourist destination.

Sicily has had a variety of difficulties recently, including organized crime, political corruption, and economic inequality. On the other hand, initiatives are being taken to deal with these problems and encourage sustainable development on the island. Sicily is still a distinct and fascinating location, with a complicated history that influences its culture and identity even today.

Geography And Climate Of Sicily

In the southernmost point of Italy, Sicily, is the largest island in the Mediterranean Sea, with a land area of 25,711 square kilometers. Its geography is distinguished by a varied topography that includes craggy mountains, undulating hills, lush valleys, and a lovely coastline.

Volcanoes and mountains

Mount Etna, an active volcano that dominates the island's eastern side, is the tallest mountain there. One of the most active volcanoes in the world, Mount Etna frequently erupts, sculpting the island's geography and history over millennia. Sicily is bordered by the Nebrodi and Madonie mountain ranges, which offer stunning scenery and rich territory for farming.

Coastline and Islands

The Mediterranean Sea encircles Sicily, which has a more than 1,000 km long coastline. The Aeolian Islands, Egadi Islands, and Pantelleria are only a few of the smaller islands that are located around the main island. The coastline offers a variety of swimming, sunbathing, and water activity opportunities, including sandy beaches, rocky coves, and sheer cliffs.

Valleys and Rivers

Sicily is crossed by several rivers, including the Simeto, Alcantara, and Belice. Citrus groves, olive groves, and vineyards can all be found in lush valleys made possible by the rivers. Several lovely valleys can be found in the island's interior, including the Noto Valley, which is renowned for its Baroque architecture and UNESCO World Heritage designation.

Climate

Sicily experiences hot, dry summers and moderate, wet winters thanks to the influence of the Mediterranean. The island is prone to warm, humid breezes from Africa because of its location amid the

Mediterranean Sea, which can bring high temperatures and sporadic storms. Summertime highs can exceed 40 degrees Celsius, while wintertime lows hardly ever fall below zero. Due to the sea breezes that reduce the temperatures, the coastal areas are often cooler than the interior.

Due to its location on the tectonic plate boundary between the African and Eurasian plates, the island is also prone to earthquakes. Sicily has a long history of seismic activity, and the island has experienced some of Italy's most devastating earthquakes. However, more recent earthquakes have had less of an impact thanks to contemporary building rules and earthquake-resistant construction techniques.

Sicily's topography and climate are a major tourist appeal and a substantial contributor to the island's economic growth. The island's natural splendor, varied topography, and warm, sunny environment make it the perfect setting for leisurely outdoor pursuits, cultural explorations, and relaxation.

Culture Of The Sicilians

Sicilians' culture is a distinctive fusion of elements from the numerous civilizations that have inhabited the island throughout history. It has a vibrant culture that is firmly based on custom, family, religion, and cuisine.

Community and Family

Sicilian culture is based on the family, and close family relationships are strongly valued. Families in Sicily are frequently big and extensive, with close ties between generations. Beyond biological relations, the term "famiglia" refers to close acquaintances and neighbors who are also regarded as family members. With close ties between neighbors and a sense of a common past and present, the community plays a significant role in Sicilian culture.

Religion

Sicilian culture is heavily influenced by religion, and the island is home to numerous stunning cathedrals, churches, and other places of worship. Catholics make up the majority of the population of Sicily, and religious celebrations and processions play a significant role in the island's cultural legacy. The Holy Week processions in Trapani and the Feast of Saint Agatha in Catania are two of Sicily's most well-known religious celebrations.

Architecture and the Arts

Sicilian art and architecture stand out for their distinctive fusion of styles from numerous eras throughout history. The Church of Santa Maria dell'Ammiraglio in Palermo and the Cathedral of San Giorgio in Ragusa are just two of the stunning Baroque structures on the island. Sicilian painters frequently depict breathtaking landscapes and seascapes in their work, which is also influenced by the island's natural beauty.

Wine and Food

Sicilian food is recognized for its rich, robust meals that emphasize using fresh, regional ingredients. The island's strong agricultural background produces a plethora of fresh produce, including citrus fruits, olives, and grapes. Fish is a staple of the Sicilian diet. Arancini, caponata, and pasta alla Norma are a few of the most well-known Sicilian foods. Nero d'Avola and Marsala are just two of the well-known varieties of Sicilian wine that are well-liked worldwide.

Dancing and music

Sicilian folk music and dance have a long history,

and they play a significant role in the island's cultural legacy. The tarantella, which is performed at weddings and other occasions, is the most well-known dance from Sicily. The zampogna, or traditional Sicilian bagpipes, and tambourine are frequently heard in traditional Sicilian music.

Generally, Sicilians have a distinctive and fascinating culture that combines history, tradition, and creativity. Visitors from all over the world continue to be inspired and enthralled by the island's rich cultural legacy, which is represented in its art, architecture, music, and gastronomy.

The Sicilians And Their Disposition To Visitors

Due to the history and culture of the island, Sicilians are renowned for being hospitable and friendly to visitors. Sicilian culture places a strong emphasis on hospitality, and tourists are frequently regarded as honored guests.

Historical Context

Sicily has a lengthy and complicated past, during which numerous civilizations have left their traces on the island. Due to the island's long history as a cultural crossroads, this history has contributed to the way Sicilians view tourists. Sicily has always accepted new influences and ideas, from the ancient Greeks and Romans to the Normans and Arabs, and this openness has extended to travelers as well.

Cultural Values

Hospitality and respect for others are highly valued in Sicilian culture. Sicilians are pleased to display their customs and way of life since they regard tourists as an opportunity to promote the island's rich culture and history. In Sicilian culture, the idea of "conviviality," which refers to the sharing of food, drink, and conversation with others, is also significant.

Hospitality

Visitors are frequently treated like family in Sicily, where hospitality is renowned. This hospitality encompasses all facets of a visitor's stay, including lodging, dining, and entertainment. Hotels and B&Bs in Sicily frequently go above and above to provide friendly and attentive service that will make guests feel at home. Also, guests are frequently encouraged to join their hosts for dinners, where they can sample the typical Sicilian fare and regional wines.

Interaction with Visitors

Sicilians often love conversing with tourists and are amicable and sociable. They are happy to provide information about their history and culture as well as suggestions for attractions and activities. Visitors can frequently anticipate being delighted by humorous stories and anecdotes because Sicilians are likewise renowned for their sense of humor and love of storytelling.

Cultural Awareness

While most visitors find Sicilians to be kind and polite, it is nevertheless vital to respect their traditions and culture. When visiting churches and other religious buildings, visitors should dress correctly and be aware of regional traditions. Respecting the environment and abiding by local rules and regulations are also very important.

Sicilians have a friendly, hospitable, and inviting attitude toward guests. Visitors to the island may anticipate being treated like honored guests and getting a close-up look at Sicily's rich cultural legacy.

CHAPTER 2

Visa & ID Requirements to visit Sicily

You'll need a current passport or national ID card from the European Union (EU) to travel to Sicily. It is still advisable to travel with your passport, even if EU nationals may enter Sicily with only their ID card. A current passport and a visa are required if you are a citizen of a non-EU nation. Depending on why you're visiting and how long you want to remain, you'll require a certain kind of visa.

A Schengen visa will probably be required for a brief visit, such as one for business or tourism. You may remain for up to 90 days in the Schengen region (which includes Italy) with this sort of visa. Your passport, a filled-out application form, and other essential papers, such as evidence of sufficient funds and travel insurance, must be submitted to apply for a Schengen visa.

A national long-term visa must be applied for if you want to remain in Sicily for more than 90 days. For visits longer than 90 days, this kind of visa is granted, and its validity is up to a year. You must submit your passport, a filled-out application form, and other needed papers, such as evidence of your ability to pay the application fee and your ability to find lodging, to apply for a national long-term visa.

Within eight days of your arrival, you must register with the local police in Sicily to show that you are here. This may be done at your hotel's front desk or the nearby police station. Your passport or another form of identification, together with documentation of your lodging and travel insurance, are required.

It is always advised to check the official website of the Italian consulate in your country for any updates or changes to the documentation needed for a trip to Sicily, including the need for a visa and an identity card.

In conclusion, if you are not a citizen of the European Union (EU), you will also require a Schengen visa for short-term visits or a national long-term visa for stays longer than 90 days to visit Sicily. Additionally, you must register with the local police within eight days of your arrival by presenting your passport or another form of photo identification, proof of lodging, and evidence of travel insurance.

Sicily travel guide 2023

Common Italian & Sicilian Phrases You Should Know

Some common Italian phrases you should know as a tourist are:

- Buongiorno (bwon-jawr-noh) - Good morning
- Buonasera (bwon-ah-seh-rah) - Good evening
- Ciao (chow) - Hello/bye
- Come va? (koh-meh vah?) - How are you?
- Grazie (grat-zee-eh) - Thank you
- Per favore (pehr fah-voh-reh) - Please
- Sì (see) - Yes
- No (noh) - No
- Non parlo Italiano (nohn par-loh ee-tah-lee-ah-noh) - I don't speak Italian
- Mi dispiace (mee dees-pee-ah-cheh) - I'm sorry
- Dove è il bagno? (doh-veh eel bahn-yoh?) - Where is the bathroom?
- Parli inglese? (par-lee een-gleh-zeh) - Do you speak English?
- Quanto costa? (kwahn-toh kohs-tah) - How much does it cost?

- Arrivederci (ah-rree-veh-dehr-chee) - Goodbye

Some common Sicilian phrases you should know as a tourist are:

- Bonjurnu (bawn-yoor-noo) - Good morning
- Bonasera (bawn-ah-seh-rah) - Good evening
- Saluti (sah-loo-tee) - Hello
- Cumu va? (koo-moo vah?) - How are you?
- Grazi (grat-zee) - Thank you
- Pi favuri (pee fah-voo-ree) - Please
- Sì (see) - Yes
- No (noh) - No
- Non parlu Sicilianu (nohn par-loo see-lee-ah-noo) - I don't speak Sicilian
- Mi dispiaci (mee dees-pee-ah-chee) - I'm sorry
- Indovi è u bagno? (een-doh-vee eh oo bah-nyo?) - Where is the bathroom?
- Parrati inglese? (pah-rah-tee een-gleh-zeh?) - Do you speak English?
- Quanto custa? (kwahn-toh koos-tah) - How much does it cost?
- Arrivederci (ah-ree-veh-dehr-chee) - Goodbye

Please note that Sicilian language is not an official language, it is a variant of Italian spoken in Sicily. And it's also important to note that there are many different dialects in Sicilian. The phrases above might be different from one region to another.

When To Visit Sicily For The Best Experience

Italy is always an excellent idea, and Sicily is a wonderful island that is no exception! However, certain months can be preferable to others if you're seeking a stress-free vacation when fewer tourists are strolling the streets and yet plenty of sunny days to enjoy.

Sicily's Weather

When you have an excellent journey planner, Sicily's weather is always perfect! The ideal time of year to go to Sicily depends on your preferred activities and weather preferences. Mild winter, blossoming spring, sun-drenched summer, and beautiful autumn all offer something unique for you to enjoy.

Sicily travel guide 2023

Sicily in the Winter and Spring

You shouldn't be concerned about the weather while planning a winter vacation to Sicily since even in the winter, the region has a significantly warmer temperature than other Italian towns. Around 50–60°F is the typical wintertime temperature. Sicily has a lot of festivals and other festive events throughout the winter, which makes it a great time to have fun and learn more about the local way of life. Bright colors are used to depict spring in Sicily. Oranges and wildflowers may be detected in the air. Sicilian spring has 66–78°F average daily highs and lows. Even though there is still a chill in the air, the island wakes from its winter slumber and comes to life.

Summertime

The main tourist season is summer when temperatures vary from 64°F at night to 93°F during the day and the sun is at its hottest. Sicily has hot, dry summers without any precipitation. You may already take advantage of the warm water and summertime sunbathing in Italy.

Fall of Sicily

The temperatures in the fall are comfortably warm, reaching up to 70°F in September and an average of 63°F in November. Late spring to early autumn is often when Sicily's weather is most pleasant for touring and sightseeing, when the landscape is at its most colorful and there is still plenty of sunlight, making it ideal for strolls through picturesque towns or relaxing days at the beach.

Temperature in Sicily:

- Winter: 50-60°F
- Spring: 60-78°F
- Summer: 77-93°F
- Fall: 55-70°F

The Number Of People Walking The Streets

The summer is without a doubt the busiest season of the year for the number of people on Sicily's streets. Since certain sites have a limited capacity, it becomes more difficult to visit particular places during the warmer months owing to an increase in tourists. In addition, lines for popular attractions like museums, restaurants, and other areas of interest seem to be becoming longer, which makes it necessary for you to waste time waiting rather than taking in Italy's extraordinary beauty.

Seasons like winter, spring, and summer are often calmer, with fewer tourists wandering the streets, making them ideal times to pause for a while and observe life in the neighborhood.

Prices

The off-peak seasons often result in reduced pricing. Unsurprisingly, costs on the island rise throughout the summer, including those for lodging, services, and, of course, the island's restaurants and cafés.

When you travel in the winter, spring, or autumn, you may not only enjoy the amazing scenery with fewer people around you, but you can also save some money since that is when you can discover the best rates on hotels and other travel essentials.

Sicily travel guide 2023

Packing And Equipment Guide To Sicily

Here are the must-bring items:

- id card with a photo and passport (be mindful of their expiration dates too)
- Products for general hygiene: toothpaste, brushes, etc (most hotels will not have these)
- Eyewear/Sun Hat (there are only 4 months a year that you will not need these)
- Simple Scarf (some churches require covered shoulders, and this is a quick fix for that)
- 2 Pin Round Electrical Adapter (many hotels will not provide these adapters)
- Map and driver's license (if renting a vehicle) (check that your license allows driving in Italy)
- Charger for Mobile Devices (you might be out from early morning to late at night)
- Currency (converted to euros) (Many establishments do not accept credit cards)
- [In Italian] Health Information Documentation Vaccinations, allergies, blood type, etc.

- a copy of your travel documents (in the event they are lost or potentially stolen)
- Walking Direction (print these off because the internet might not be readily available)
- Sunscreen (particularly if you are intending to come to May-September) (especially if you are planning to arrive May-September)
- The Treatment Of Jellyfish Stings (you might encounter jellyfish on some beaches)
- Italian-language Pocket Dictionary (Only a few individuals in Palermo speak English)
- Compact Umbrella (if you come in the winter months)
- Camera (there will be a lot you want photographs of here) (there will be a lot you want pictures of here)
- Portable Backpack (useful to carry everything on day trips of sightseeing)
- a mosquito repellent (especially annoying during the summer months)
- Bathing suit (if you plan to enjoy the beaches during the summer)
- Trekking Boots (if you intend to climb Mt. Etna or other mountainous areas)

Sicily travel guide 2023

By following this packing and equipment guide, you'll be well-prepared for your trip to Sicily and ready to explore all the island has to offer.

CHAPTER 3

Interesting Things To Do In Sicily

Sicily is well-known for its breathtaking coastline, historic sites, and delectable cuisine. Seeing ancient Greek and Roman sites and relaxing on some of Europe's most stunning beaches are just a few of the exciting things that visitors to Sicily may do.

Mount Etna, an active volcano that dominates the eastern section of the island, is one of Sicily's main tourist destinations. To admire the views of the surrounding area, visitors can either trek to the mountain's summit or use a cable car. Several wonderful cities and villages may be found in the vicinity of Mount Etna, including Taormina, which is renowned for its breathtaking sea vistas, lovely gardens, and old Greek theater.

The Valley of the Temples, a UNESCO World Heritage Site near the town of Agrigento, is another must-see destination in Sicily. The Temple of Concordia and the Temple of Zeus are two of the best-preserved Greek ruins in existence, both of which may be found in the Valley of the Temples. The ruins are accessible to visitors on foot or by guided tour.

Sicily is renowned for having stunning beaches, including the sands of Cefalù on the island's northern coast. Cefalù is a charming coastal community renowned for its pristine waters and ancient Norman Cathedral. Another well-liked vacation spot for beachgoers is the group of seven islands known as the Aeolian Islands, which are situated off the northern coast of Sicily. The islands are renowned for their breathtaking volcanic vistas, glistening waters, and lovely beaches.

Visitors can enjoy Sicily's rich history and culture in addition to its natural beauty. The vibrant metropolis of Palermo, the capital of Sicily, is home to numerous historic sites, such as the Palermo Cathedral, the Quattro Canti, and the Palermo Royal Palace. The Temple of Athena and the Amphitheater are just two of the significant Greek and Roman ruins that can be found at Syracuse, an ancient city on Sicily's southeast coast.

Sicily travel guide 2023

Sicily is renowned for its delectable cuisine, which combines Mediterranean and Italian flavors. Tourists can eat regional favorites including cannoli, caponata, and arancini, which are deep-fried rice balls (a sweet pastry filled with ricotta cheese). Sicily is home to several vibrant street markets where tourists can buy local specialties including fresh fish and veggies.

Last but not least, Sicily is a fantastic location for outdoor enthusiasts, offering a variety of activities like hiking, cycling, and diving. The island's rough terrain is ideal for hiking and cycling, and its crystal-clear seas make it a well-liked spot for diving and snorkeling.

Finally, Sicily is an intriguing and varied travel location that offers something for everyone. There is a lot to see and do in Sicily, whether your interests are taking in the beauty of a gorgeous beach, discovering historical ruins, or enjoying the local cuisine.

Sicily travel guide 2023

Top Attractions To Visit In Sicily

Here are some of the top attractions to explore in Sicily:

1. Aeolian Islands

Off Sicily's northeastern coast in the Tyrrhenian Sea, the Aeolian Islands are a group of volcanic islands. Lipari, Vulcano, Salina, Stromboli, Filicudi, Alicudi, and Panarea are the seven major islands that make up the archipelago. The islands are well-known for their untamed environments, black sand beaches, and pristine waterways.

The biggest and most populated island, Lipari, also serves as the administrative and port hub for the whole archipelago. The ancient Greek city of Lipari, which was established in the eighth century BC, is one of its many well-known archaeological monuments. Salina is well-known for its vineyards and Malvasia wine production, whilst the island of Vulcano is well-known for its active volcano and hot springs.

As the "Lighthouse of the Mediterranean," Stromboli is the only volcano in the world with a nearly constant eruption.
Since they are the furthest away and least populated of the islands, Filicudi and Alicudi are well-liked by hikers and environment lovers. The smallest and most exclusive island is Panarea, which is renowned for its upscale hotels and eateries.

Tourists who want to enjoy the natural beauty of the islands and the local culture often go to the Aeolian Islands, which are also UNESCO World Heritage Sites. In addition to enjoying the local food and nightlife, tourists may enjoy hiking, swimming, snorkeling, and diving.

Sicily travel guide 2023

2. Mount Etna

On the eastern side of the Italian island of Sicily stands Mount Etna, an active stratovolcano. It is one of the most active volcanoes in the world and the tallest volcano in Europe, rising beyond 10,000 feet. With records reaching as far back as 1500 BC, the volcano has a complicated and lengthy history of eruptions.

Etna is a shield volcano with regular, non-explosive eruptions and a wide, gently sloping slope. The volcano's composition alternates between layers of lava and ash, and it contains several craters and vents that may cause simultaneous eruptions. The

Northeast Crater, Central Crater, and South-East Crater are the volcano's three primary summit craters.

Known for its beautiful vistas and challenging climbing paths that lead to the top, Mount Etna is a well-liked tourist attraction. Visitors may also go on guided trips to the volcano's crater, where they can see the lava flows and volcanic activities that are now in progress. Depending on the weather, the volcano also provides a range of outdoor activities such as mountain biking, skiing, and snowboarding.

The region and the local inhabitants have both been significantly impacted by Etna's eruptions. Unique landscapes and ecosystems, including woods, vineyards, and orchards, have been created as a result of the volcano's activity. Since volcanic ash may be gathered and utilized industrially, the eruption also has a financial effect.

International treaties have been made to safeguard the ecological and cultural assets of Mount Etna, which is also a UNESCO World Heritage Site. Numerous institutes and observatories keep an eye on it since it is a crucial location for scientific research as well as to track its activities and identify possible dangers.

3. Greek Theatre of Taormina

The Greek Theatre of Taormina often referred to as the Teatro Antico di Taormina, is a historic theater situated in the Italian town of Taormina on the island of Sicily. It is regarded as one of the most exquisite and well-maintained antique theaters in the whole world. The theater was created by the Greeks in the third century BC, and it was subsequently extended by the Romans.

Around 5,000 people can fit in the theater, which is carved into the side of a hill and offers a breathtaking view of the sea and the surroundings. It still serves as a venue for shows, concerts, and cultural events today, making it a striking example of old engineering and architectural design.

White marble makes up the theater, and stunning statues and frescoes adorn the stage. The auditorium's (seating area) two floors are separated by a wooden ceiling that served as its original roof. VIPs were only allowed on the top level, while regular folks were only allowed on the bottom level.

One of the most significant historical and cultural landmarks in Sicily is the Greek Theatre of Taormina, which is a UNESCO World Heritage Site. Through guided tours, visitors may examine the theater and discover more about its history and importance. The theater is accessible to the general public and is a well-liked tourist spot, noted for its stunning vistas, extensive history, and cultural activities.

It is also renowned for its breathtaking snow-capped Mount Etna background, which acts as a natural stage for the annual Taormina Festival, which is held in the summer and involves classical music, dance, and theatrical events.

4. Selinunte Archaeological Park

One of the greatest and most significant ancient Greek archaeological sites in Sicily, Italy, is the Selinunte Archaeological Park. It may be found close to Castelvetrano on the island's southwest shore. Selinunte was one of the most significant Greek colonies in Sicily and its remnants may be seen in the park.

The Greeks established Selinunte in the seventh century BC, and in the fifth century BC, it reached its height of prosperity. The city was divided into several communities and was fortified with walls and towers on all sides. The city was also the location of several temples, including the Temple of Concordia, the Temple of Zeus, and the Temple of Hera.

The park is home to several historic buildings, notably the acropolis, which served as the city's religious and political hub. The theater, agora, and other remnants of the city may all be explored by tourists. There is a museum inside the park that houses a variety of artifacts and sculptures uncovered there.

The Selinunte Archaeological Park is one of Sicily's most significant cultural and historical monuments and is a UNESCO World Heritage Site. In addition to exploring the park, visitors may take guided tours to learn about its importance and history. Known for its stunning vistas, extensive history, and cultural activities, the park is accessible to the public and is a well-liked tourist attraction.

A park is a fantastic place to observe the ruins of the ancient Greek civilization that once existed in Sicily and to get a sense of the size and significance of the city in prehistoric times. The park is a superb illustration of the blending of Sicilian local culture with Greek influences that occurred on the island.

5. Monreale Cathedral

The stunning ancient cathedral known as the Monreale Cathedral, also called the Cathedral of the Assumption of the Virgin Mary, is situated in the town of Monreale, which is a suburb of Palermo, Sicily, Italy. King William II, sometimes referred to as William the Good, erected the cathedral as a reminder of the Norman conquest of Sicily in the 12th century.

A combination of styles and influences can be seen throughout the cathedral, which is a masterpiece of Norman-Arab-Byzantine construction. Intricate mosaics and paintings that are some of the most stunning and well-preserved specimens of medieval art can be seen within the cathedral. The façade of the cathedral is distinguished by its Romanesque architecture with a blend of Arabic features.

The mosaics, which span an area of more than 6,000 square meters, include images from the Old and New Testaments as well as from Christ's and Mary's lives. The mosaics, which are created from tiny glass and ceramic tesserae, are regarded as one of the most significant works of Byzantine art in the western world.

The Monreale Cathedral is one of Sicily's most significant cultural and historical landmarks and is a UNESCO World Heritage Site. Through guided tours, visitors may see the cathedral's interior and enjoy its artwork, including mosaics, frescoes, and sculptures. The cathedral is accessible to the general public and is a well-liked vacation spot because of its stunning scenery, fascinating history, and cultural activities.

Another significant religious location is the Monreale Cathedral, which continues to host religious services and masses. A modest museum with liturgical costumes, goldsmith work, and pottery that were used in the cathedral is located in the cathedral's lovely cloister, which is well worth seeing.

6. Villa Romana del Casale

The village of Piazza Armerina, in the geographic center of Sicily, Italy, is home to the historic Roman villa known as the Villa Romana del Casale. The villa was constructed during the Roman Empire's 4th century AD and now is regarded as one of the most significant and well-preserved specimens of Roman art and architecture in existence.

The villa is a substantial structure with a floor area of more than 35,000 square meters, and a Roman aristocratic family most likely utilized it for hunting and recreation. A huge courtyard, peristyle, hot bath, and several rooms and hallways, many of which are mosaic-decorated, are among the villa's many architectural characteristics.

Some of the most exquisite and well-preserved specimens of Roman art may be found in the mosaics, which span an area of more than 3,500 square meters. They portray a variety of scenarios, including sports, daily life, hunting, fishing, and other activities, as well as mythical and religious themes. The mosaics are known for their elaborate patterns and vivid colors and are fashioned of tiny stone and glass tesserae.

One of Sicily's most significant cultural and historical landmarks, the Villa Romana del Casale is a UNESCO World Heritage Site. With the help of guides, guests may visit the estate and take in its artwork, architecture, mosaics, and frescoes. The villa is accessible to the general public and is a well-liked tourist site, recognized for its stunning vistas, extensive history, and cultural activities.

A wonderful illustration of the grandeur and wealth of the Roman elite's way of life, as well as the blending of Roman and Sicilian culture, the Villa Romana del Casale offers an insight into the routines, rituals, and traditions of ancient Roman society. The mosaics are one of the world's biggest and most comprehensive collections of Roman mosaics, and they represent a particularly significant and distinctive aspect of the villa.

7. Valley of the Temples

Agrigento, a town on Sicily's southern coast, is home to the archaeological monument known as the Valley of the Temples. Ancient Greek temple ruins from the fifth century BC, when Agrigento was known as the city of Akragas, one of the most significant and rich Greek colonies in Sicily, may be found at this location.

A UNESCO World Heritage Site, the Valley of the Temples is regarded as one of Sicily's most significant cultural and historical monuments. Seven temples were formerly located here, and three of them—the Temple of Hera, sometimes called the Temple of Concordia, the Temple of Heracles, and the Temple of Olympian Zeus—have the finest remaining structures. Some of the world's finest surviving examples of classical Greek architecture are these temples.

Along with the museum, which showcases a variety of antiques and sculptures discovered at the site, the site also has remnants of other buildings, including the stoa, the agora, and the theater. Guided tours are available to let visitors explore the location and discover its importance and history.

Popular tourist attractions like the Valley of the Temples are renowned for their breathtaking scenery, fascinating pasts, and cultural activities. Visitors may take in the expansive views of the surrounding countryside while admiring the majestic Doric columns and other ancient Greek architectural characteristics of the temples. The temples are also a fantastic illustration of how Sicily's local Sicilian culture and Greek civilization merged.

It is a rare chance to witness the ruins of the ancient Greek civilization in Sicily and to understand the size and significance of the city in prehistoric times. The Valley of the Temples is also a fantastic place to learn about the religion, culture, and society of the ancient Greeks. The region is a wonderful spot to wander and unwind since it is also surrounded by lovely gardens.

8. Royal Palace and Palatine Chapel

In the Italian region of Sicily's capital city of Palermo are the Royal Palace and Palatine Chapel. The palace was built in the ninth century during the Arab-Norman era and served as the primary home of the Sicilian Norman rulers. Later, the Normans, Swabians, and Aragonese kings among others extended and altered the palace.

The palace is a collection of structures, which also includes the Palatine Chapel, several courtyards, and gardens. The palace is distinguished by the variety of architectural styles that represent the many eras of its construction and alteration. A wide central courtyard, a peristyle, a throne chamber, and a private chapel are some of the characteristics of the palace.

Within the palace sits the Palatine Chapel, a modest yet stunning chapel. It was constructed in the 12th century by King Roger II and is regarded as one of the world's most significant examples of Arab-Norman architecture. The chapel is decorated with elaborate mosaics, frescoes, and sculptures that show scenes from both the Old and New Testaments as well as from the lives of Christ and the Virgin Mary.

One of the most significant historical and cultural landmarks in Sicily is the Royal Palace and Palatine Chapel. Through guided tours, guests may look at the palace and enjoy its artwork, mosaics, and sculptures. The palace is accessible to the general public and is a well-liked tourist site, recognized for its stunning vistas, extensive history, and cultural activities.

As a reflection of the many cultures and civilizations that have reigned over Sicily throughout the ages, the palace and chapel are renowned for their synthesis of several architectural forms. The chapel and the castle serve as significant examples of how Sicily's medieval history saw the mingling of many cultures and faiths.

9. Teatro Massimo

Palermo, Sicily, Italy is home to the Teatro Massimo, an opera venue. One of the biggest and most significant opera houses in Italy and across Europe, the theater was constructed in the late 19th century. The architect Giovanni Battista Filippo Basile, who created the theater, modeled it on the Paris Opera House.

The theater, which can accommodate around 1,400 people, is renowned for its stunning architecture and furnishings. Complex sculptures, stuccos, and frescoes are used to embellish the theater. Apollo, the god of music and poetry, triumphs in a fresco that is painted on the theater's ceiling. The stage, which measures 60 meters by 18 meters, is one of the biggest in Italy and all of Europe.

Known for its stunning vistas, extensive history, and cultural activities, the Teatro Massimo is a well-liked tourist attraction. Through guided tours, visitors may examine the theater and enjoy its design, frescoes, sculptures, and stuccos. Opera, ballet, and classical music events are held in the theater, which is also home to the Orchestra Sinfonica Siciliana and the Coro del Teatro Massimo.

As one of Sicily's most significant cultural and historical landmarks, the Teatro Massimo is also a UNESCO World Heritage Site. In addition to being a symbol of Palermo, it is also the biggest theater in Italy and one of the biggest in all of Europe. The theater has hosted several renowned opera singers, conductors, and performers throughout the years. It also serves as a key location for the yearly Palermo Opera Season.

10. Mondello Beach

Popular beach Mondello Beach is situated in Mondello, a village outside of Palermo, Sicily, Italy. The beach is renowned for its crystal-clear seas, fine golden sand, and lovely surroundings. It is surrounded by luxuriant Mediterranean greenery, and a promenade dotted with eateries, cafés, and ice cream shops run behind it.

A well-liked location for swimming, tanning, and water activities including windsurfing, kitesurfing, and sailing is Mondello Beach. Because it provides a range of kid-friendly activities, such as playgrounds and inflatable games, it is also a well-liked family attraction. A broad variety of amenities, such as umbrellas, lounge chairs, and showers, are available at the beach.

In addition to its stunning Art Nouveau-style structures, many of which have been transformed into hotels and flats, Mondello Beach is also well-known for them. The beach is also home to a small fishing community where tourists may sample regional seafood delicacies and purchase fresh fish.

Both residents and visitors like visiting the beach, which is conveniently accessible by public transit. The beach is still a fantastic spot to unwind and take in the stunning Mediterranean water, even if it may become fairly busy during the summer.

Mondello Beach is a great site for anyone who wishes to get away from the city, spend a day at the beach, and take in the stunning Art Nouveau architecture of the nearby buildings. The Capo Gallo Natural Reserve and the Parco della Favorita are only a few of the nearby attractions in addition to the beach.

11. Zingaro Reserve

The northwest coast of Sicily, Italy, is home to the Zingaro Reserve, a protected natural area. It was founded in 1981 and is renowned for its stunning beaches, rugged cliffs, and Mediterranean flora. The reserve is 7.2 square kilometers in size and is known for its varied and pristine natural surroundings.

Sicily travel guide 2023

The reserve is home to a broad diversity of plant and animal life, including Mediterranean shrubs, wildflowers, and herbs, as well as animals, birds, and reptiles. Some endangered species, like the peregrine falcon and the European eagle owl, call it home.

Visitors may engage in a range of activities in the reserve, including hiking, swimming, snorkeling, and bird-watching. Several hiking routes take you to the reserve's most breathtaking locations, such as the renowned Tonnara, a little fishing town, and the Cala Marinella, a gorgeous beach with clean seas.

Additionally, visitors may take boat excursions to explore the reserve's shoreline and take in the stunning scenery.

Nature enthusiasts, hikers, and beachgoers often visit the Zingaro Reserve. It's a fantastic location for anybody who wants to see northwest Sicily's coastline area and get a taste of the island's distinctive natural and cultural history. It's a remarkable illustration of how nature and human culture can live together and of how local communities may gain from environmental preservation.

Numerous organizations and observatories keep an eye on it to study its biodiversity and ecosystems since it is a crucial location for scientific research. To maintain its natural legacy, international agreements and legislation have designated the Reserve as a significant location for conservation.

12. Palermo Cathedral

The Cathedral of Saint Mary of the Admiral, usually referred to as the Palermo Cathedral, is a stunning medieval cathedral that can be found in the center of

Palermo, Sicily, Italy. The cathedral was constructed by the Normans in the 12th century, and it is regarded as one of the most significant instances of Norman-Arab-Byzantine architecture in the whole globe.

Several chapels, a cloister, and a bell tower are all part of the cathedral's expansive complex of structures. The cathedral's façade is distinguished by its Norman-style construction, which incorporates certain Arabic design features. The interior is covered with complex mosaics, frescoes, and sculptures, which are some of the most stunning and well-preserved specimens of medieval art in the whole world.

One of the cathedral's highlights is its mosaics, which were created in the Byzantine style and include scenes from the Old and New Testaments as well as from the lives of Christ and the Virgin Mary. The mosaics, which are created from tiny glass and ceramic tesserae, are regarded as one of the most significant works of Byzantine art in the western world.

Known for its stunning vistas, extensive history, and cultural activities, the Palermo Cathedral is a well-liked tourist attraction. Through guided tours, visitors may see the cathedral's interior and enjoy its artwork, including mosaics, frescoes, and sculptures. The cathedral is accessible to the general public and continues to be used for religious services and masses.

One of the most significant historical and cultural landmarks in Sicily is the Palermo Cathedral, which is also a UNESCO World Heritage Site. The cathedral is a wonderful example of how many cultures and faiths were assimilated throughout the Middle Ages in Sicily, and it offers a wonderful chance to see the mingling of Norman, Arabic, and Byzantine traditions.

13. Castello Maniace

In Syracuse, Sicily, Italy, there is a castle called Castello Maniace, sometimes called Fortezza Maniace. Frederick II, commonly known as Frederick II of Hohenstaufen, the Holy Roman Emperor, constructed it in the thirteenth century. The fortress bears the name of George Maniakes, a Byzantine commander who overran Syracuse in the eleventh century. The fort was constructed as an anti-attack barrier and the emperor's military garrison.

The architectural design of the castle is distinctive, combining Byzantine and medieval features. With four corner towers and a central courtyard, it is square. Local limestone was used to construct the walls, which are substantial and thick. A unique feature for castles in the period, the castle was built to be self-sufficient and had its water supply.

The castle fulfilled a variety of functions throughout history. It was a military barracks and a storehouse before being utilized as a jail during the Spanish rule of Sicily in the 16th century. A look into the past of the city and the surrounding area is available to tourists at this well-liked tourist attraction today. In addition, the castle provides stunning views of Syracuse, the countryside, and the ocean. Additionally, guests are welcome to visit the castle's many chambers, which include the chapel, the jail cells, and the cisterns.

14. Catacombe dei Cappuccini

The Catacombs of the Capuchins, or Catacombe dei Cappuccini in Italian, are a group of underground graves in Palermo, Sicily. They were constructed in the 16th century by Capuchin monks, who belonged to the Capuchin Order of Minor Friars in the Roman Catholic Church. According to the traditions of the period, which mandated that the deceased be either on church property or within walking distance of it, the dead were interred in the catacombs.

In the strange and unsettling Catacombs of the Capuchins, the dead are not interred in the earth but rather left exposed on the walls. Around 8,000 people's bones are located in the catacombs, which have five levels and a chapel on each. The remains were preserved for a long time because of a unique method of mummification. In addition, there is a sizable collection of funeral objects in the catacombs, including clothes, jewelry, and other personal belongings.

The Catacombs of the Capuchins are a well-liked tourist attraction and are regarded as one of Palermo's most significant historical landmarks. Visitors may tour the catacombs and see the mummified remains of priests, monks, and lords as well as men, women, and children from various socioeconomic groups. It's a gruesome yet intriguing attraction that provides insight into the social mores of the period. Visitors may take guided tours of the catacombs every day, and they can choose from a variety of languages.

Sicily travel guide 2023

15. Spiaggia di San Vito lo Capo

The Catacombs of the Capuchins, or Catacombe dei Cappuccini in Italian, are a group of underground graves in Palermo, Sicily. They were constructed in the 16th century by Capuchin monks, who belonged to the Capuchin Order of Minor Friars in the Roman Catholic Church. According to the traditions of the period, which mandated that the deceased be either on church property or within walking distance of it, the dead were interred in the catacombs.

In the strange and unsettling Catacombs of the Capuchins, the dead are not interred in the earth but rather left exposed on the walls. Around 8,000 people's bones are located in the catacombs, which have five levels and a chapel on each. The remains were preserved for a long time because of a unique method of mummification. In addition, there is a sizable collection of funeral objects in the catacombs, including clothes, jewelry, and other personal belongings.

The Catacombs of the Capuchins are a well-liked tourist attraction and are regarded as one of Palermo's most significant historical landmarks. Visitors may tour the catacombs and see the mummified remains of priests, monks, and lords as well as men, women, and children from various socioeconomic groups. It's a gruesome yet intriguing attraction that provides insight into the social mores of the period. Visitors may take guided tours of the catacombs every day, and they can choose from a variety of languages.

Recommended Hotels To Lodge In Sicily

1. Belmond Grand Hotel Timeo

The Belmond Grand Hotel Timeo is a well-liked getaway for couples and families, nestled among Mount Tauro's cliffs in Taormina, Sicily. You'll discover neutral color schemes, hardwood floors, marble baths, vivid accent linens, and throw cushions, as well as in-room conveniences like free Wi-Fi and iPod docking stations, in each of the property's 71 guest rooms and suites.

Along with balconies or patios, rooms have panoramic views of the harbor and Mount Etna's metropolis. The Literary Terrace & Bar and the three restaurants on the resort, which focus on Sicilian and Mediterranean cuisine, also provide magnificent views. Several gardens, a spa, and a heated pool are among the other on-site facilities. The Belmond Villa Sant'Andrea, the hotel's sister property, also has a private beach that can be reached by free shuttle service from the Belmond Grand Hotel Timeo. But keep in mind that the Belmond Grand Hotel Timeo is closed from mid-November to mid-March every year.

2. Hotel Gutkowski, Ortigia, Syracuse

Hotel Gutkowski is a charming boutique hotel with a soft blue color on the Lungomare Levante, which is an island off the coast of Ortigia. It consists of two former fishermen's cottages that have been exquisitely refurbished to provide 26 distinct rooms designed in a simple coastal style with select pieces of designer furniture. Two seaside patios are available, as well as a small ground-floor restaurant that offers contemporary Sicilian cuisine till late. The breakfast buffet is delectable and includes baked pastries and freshly squeezed juice. For those who want to explore Ortigia's island, options include free bike rental.

3. Belmond Villa Sant'Andrea, Taormina

The regal beauty of this once privately held mansion is still present. Large floor-to-ceiling windows accentuate views of the hotel's beach and subtropical gardens, while modern artwork gives traditionally designed rooms a fresh look. Visitors may use the amenities of the sister hotel Timeo, which has a heated infinity pool, a wellness center with an outdoor pavilion for massages, and other amenities. The informal beach bar provides beverages and light fare all day, while the Oliviero terrace restaurant specializes in regional cuisine, notably seafood. In the evenings, live music is also played at the beach bar.

4. Capofaro Malvasia Hotel & Resort, Salina, Aeolian Islands

A few whitewashed Aeolian homes on the greenest of the Aeolian Islands have been transformed into a chic, minimalist refuge among the Tasca d'Almerita vineyards at the base of two extinct volcanoes. There are 21 rooms with sea views, each with a patio, whitewashed walls, and neutral furnishings. A lighthouse is getting a couple of more rooms. Along with the opportunity to sample Malvasia wine, the image is completed with an infinity pool, tennis facilities, and fine cuisine. Throughout the year, regular cooking, yoga, and pilates classes are scheduled.

5. Casa Talìa, Modica

A hipster retreat has been created by architects Marco Guinto and his wife Viviana Haddad in a charming Baroque village an hour from Syracuse using traditional tiles, local stone, and eccentric furnishings. Ten uniquely built rooms with balconies or patios are housed in the renovated fishermen's huts. Delicious breakfasts, featuring Sicilian pastries, are provided in a dining room carved out of rock. Additional amenities include the supply of picnic hampers and visits to nearby locations where you may partake in them.

6. Monaci delle Terre Nere, Zafferana

Located 20 miles from Catania, this chic eco-retreat is ideal for those who want to relax by the pool or the sea, have a massage, and sometimes hike Mount Etna's slopes. With the addition of modern art and designer furniture, the renovated "palmento," an antique winery with numerous authentic Sicilian elements, comes alive. The apartments are elegant, have lava stone walls and worn timbers, and have wood-burning stoves, which are necessary for the winter. Visit the restaurant, which provides fresh, in-season food, if you're hungry. It even incorporates elements from the hotel's organic farm, which is a thoughtful addition.

7. Grand Hotel Minareto, Syracuse

The Minareto is a massive complex of rooms, suites, and villas located outside of town on the border of the Plemmirio Nature Reserve. It has breathtaking views of Ortigia and is surrounded by nature (seven miles away). All of the well-appointed rooms have patios, and bigger suites have direct access to a sandy beach. In addition to a pool, there is a hot tub terrace, as well as sports and spa amenities. A refined à la carte menu centered on regional foods and traditional specialties is available at La Terrazza Latomie and The Nesos Restaurant.

8. Giuggiulena, Syracuse

An oceanfront B&B on a cliff is called Giuggiulena. Even though it only has seven rooms, each one is furnished with trendy, colorful pieces that also include vintage elements to give the space more personality. The patio is the ideal location to enjoy the breathtaking views, particularly when sipping an apero. You may chow down on a sizable breakfast buffet in the morning while the Jonico restaurant provides everything from pizza to traditional fare. When you're not enjoying the delectable fresh Italian cuisine, you can keep yourself busy with Solarium Zen's sunbed patio and complimentary bike rentals.

9. The Ashbee, Taormina

The Ashbee is a tastefully renovated big home with lots of marble and ambiance, set on lovely grounds. Twenty-five bright, spacious rooms, some with patios or terraces overlooking the sea, are understatedly furnished with fine antiques. If you can pull yourself away from the infinity pool in between, additional food and drinks are offered at a garden bar.
The panoramic rooftop Terrace Bar provides an outstanding buffet breakfast and pre-dinner cocktails. For supper, a more formal restaurant offers traditional Italian fare.

10. Alma Hotel

The household-run In the heart of Palermo's old district lies a modest jewel called Alma. Owners Paolo and Antonella and their employees provide exceptional customer service by going above and beyond to make you feel at home and provide advice, guidance, and knowledge. Although this motel is situated in a nameless building, inside it is bright and modern. The old city is featured on the walls of each of the seven available rooms, and breakfast options include handmade cannoli or cassata. Although the hotel doesn't have a restaurant or bar, there are several excellent restaurants outside the front door.

These are just a few of the recommended hotels for visitors to lodge in Sicily. There are many other hotels to choose from, depending on your preferences and budget. When planning your trip to Sicily, be sure to research different hotels and read reviews from other travelers to find the best option for you.

Suggested Restaurants To Eat In Sicily

The delicious traditional and contemporary tastes served at these fantastic Sicilian eateries help to distinguish the island's food from that of the rest of the Italian mainland. Sicily as it is known today is the result of a protracted and intricate past that took place inside one of Italy's most spectacular geographical settings. Fusion cuisine exhibits the natural and cultural wealth of the region. The island's special cuisine is influenced by Italian, Greek, Arab, Spanish, and French cuisine.

Some of Sicily's top eateries use local markets' fresh produce and seafood that has been caught on neighboring quaysides. These ingredients are transformed into something unique in the kitchens of these fantastic restaurants in Sicily by some of its most talented and creative chefs. During your trip to a Mediterranean island, have a look at these top recommendations for dining in Sicily.

1. La Madia

On Sicily's southern coast near Licata, there is a two Michelin-starred restaurant called La Madia. The restaurant gets its stars since its chef offers flavorful and inventive Sicilian meals. He serves it in a chic, stylish eating area with a simple design that guarantees that the focus is on the cuisine, just where it should be.

The chef's secret ingredient is always present in every dish: recollections. The experience aims to simulate island living regularly. You may choose from items on its a la carte menu, such as smoked

cod and honey-glazed pigeon. When you feel a little overpowered by the inventive options, there are also several tasting menus available.
Located at Corso Filippo Re Capriata, 22, 92027 Licata AG, Italy

Opens: Monday and Wednesday–Saturday from 1 pm to 2.30 pm and from 8 pm to 10 pm, Sunday from 8 pm to 10 pm

Phone: +39 09 2277 1443
2. Duomo Ristorante

The neighboring San Giorgio church serves as the inspiration for Ragusa's Duomo restaurant, which has two Michelin stars. You'll remember the hilltop city's historical landmarks, scenic vistas, and culinary experience for a very long time.

Here, analyzing and reinventing the classics are the main points. In the expert hands of one of Sicily's most skilled chefs, go on an unforgettable trip through the landscape and culture of this diverse island. The three essential ingredients of every meal are oil, wheat, and salt, albeit the menus fluctuate with the seasons. As a starter, try the various fish of

the day from Duomo or the crispy fried tuma (white cheese) with honey. For a main dish, try macaroni with fried eggplant and Florentine sirloin steak.
Located at Ibla, Via Capitano Bocchieri, 31, 97100 Ragusa RG, Italy

Opens: Monday from 7.30 pm to 11.30 pm, Tuesday–Saturday from 12.30 pm to 2 pm and from 7.30 pm to 10.30 pm

Phone: +39 09 3265 1265

3. Otto Geleng

A famous Sicilian restaurant named Otto Geleng is named after a German painter who made Taormina his adoptive home and was enamored by it. This little eatery is located in the upscale Belmond Grand Hotel Timeo. You may enjoy the same vista from its terrace that Geleng did.

You'll be fed traditional Mediterranean food that combines tradition and innovation under the supervision of its renowned chef. Locally obtained resources from the land and the sea are used to prepare dishes. The degustation menu of Otto

Geleng includes red mullet with artichokes, foie gras, and passionfruit, tuna belly with cooked must and pickled cabbage, and ravioli with caviar and porcini mushrooms.

Located at Via Teatro Greco, 59, 98039 Taormina ME, Italy

Opens: Thursday–Sunday from 8 pm to 10 pm (closed Mondays to Wednesdays)

4. La Capinera

La Capinera, a restaurant in Taormina, has a Michelin star and a well-deserved reputation for culinary excellence because of its exquisite but straightforward approach to fine dining. The chef's inventiveness, which can be seen in each meal, is based on the elements of sea, air, land, and fire.

Following paccheri pasta sautéed with clams and prawns and slow-roasted lamb in a Marsala wine sauce, there comes warm pistachio cake and orange mousse. Eat outside on the patio while admiring the Ionian Sea in the summer. Reserve a seat in our warm dining area during cold weather..

Located at Via Nazionale, 177, 98039 Taormina ME, Italy

Opens: Tuesday–Sunday from 12.30 pm to 2.30 pm and from 7.30 pm to 10.30 pm (closed on Mondays)

Phone: +39 33 8158 8013

5. I Pupi

Thanks to its celebrated chef who approaches the kitchen with love and vigor, I Pupi, which is Italian for "The Puppets," is deserving of its Michelin star. The street culinary culture, enduring family traditions, and the plentiful local products of Sicily serve as the inspiration for beautifully presented meals.

To counteract the intensity of color and brightness of the food on the dish, the décor is monochromatic and simple. Try I Pup's version of stigghiola, a specialty of Sicily. Playfully substituting tuna and squid for the traditional street food's lamb and leeks.

Located at Via del Cavaliere, 59, 90011 Bagheria PA, Italy
Opens: Daily from 12.30 pm to 2 pm and from 7.30 pm to 10.30 pm

Phone: +39 09 1902 579

6. Osteria Ballarò

On the outskirts of Palermo's historic Jewish district, Osteria Ballar is an Italian restaurant. It used to be the stables of the ancient Palazzo Cattolica. It promotes the slow food movement in this evocative environment, which has exposed brick walls and an exquisite vaulted ceiling.

Every kind of meat, seafood, cheese, and wine is native to Sicily, with the majority coming from tiny artisan producers. Expect a constantly changing menu since the fruit is exclusively seasonal. The handmade pasta tortelloni with buffalo ricotta cheese and tenerumi are among the meals that are highly recommended (Sicilian broadleaf vegetables).

Located at Via Calascibetta, 25, 90133 Palermo PA, Italy

Opens: Daily from noon to 3 pm and from 7 pm to 11 pm

Phone: +39 09 1326 488

7. Viri Ku C'e

Southeast Sicily's Vittoria is home to the beachfront restaurant Viri Ku C'e. It's a terrific spot to eat seafood after spending the day at Scoglitti's sandy beach since it's just across the street from the beach. Come with an open mind and an empty stomach since the fixed-price menu's offerings vary every day depending on what has been caught.

Clams, oysters, mussels, scallops, langoustines, and shrimp may be served as an appetizer, while handmade pasta and grilled fish may be served as a main course. The fish may then be fileted for you at the table. Everything at Viri Ku C'e is finished with refreshing lemon sorbet.

Located at Via Riviera Gela , 13/a, 97019 Scoglitti, Vittoria, RG, Italy

Opens: Daily from 1 pm to 3 pm and from 8 pm to midnight

Phone: +39 09 3298 0016

8. Osteria Da Rita

Genuine Sicilian cuisine is served in large servings at Osteria Da Rita in Taormina. Since it is nestled away on a peaceful street, it is pleasant to eat outdoors at one of the tables covered in cherry red gingham tablecloths.

Both the wine served with it and the food are undeniably Sicilian. At Osteria Da Rita, there is a wide selection of straightforward classics. It's a welcoming and relaxed environment. Customers are asked to sing along and are given free rein over the music selection.

Located at Via Calapitrulli, 3, 98039 Taormina ME, Italy

Phone: +39 09 4268 1015

9. Manna Noto

With its Mediterranean cuisine and relaxing atmosphere, Manna Noto is a restaurant in Noto that delivers a feast for the senses. Once inside, you'll discover a lovely space with spectacular lighting and eccentric accents. The lighted soda sign above the bar and a wall made of wine bottles are notable features. A room that was once the bottom level of a palace is now updated with a sleek, modern aesthetic.

Locally produced ingredients provide straightforward meals that just need the chef's love of cooking to become something special. They are just as well arranged as everything around them. A typical Sicilian dish or some grilled fish are also good choices. The handmade pasta from Manna Noto is also a top pick.

Located at Via Rocco Pirri, 19, 96017 Noto SR, Italy

Opens: Hours vary by season

Phone: +39 09 3183 6051

10. Gourmet 32

Sicilian cuisine is served often at Gourmet 32 in Taormina. Its culinary team transforms traditional Sicilian cuisine into modern versions.
Consider ordering the swordfish from your area with capers and olives or the duck breast with a Sicilian citrus sauce. Finish off the meal with a rich tiramisu or an almond parfait.

If you're stuck for a choice, there are tasting menus with meat, fish, and vegetarian options. If possible, dine outside on the covered patio to enjoy the sights and ambiance. The old Greco-Roman amphitheater known as Teatro Antico di Taormina is located to the east of Gourmet 32.

Located at Via Bagnoli Croci, 31, 98039 Taormina ME, Italy

Opens: Daily from noon to 3 pm and from 6 pm to 11 pm

Phone: +39 38 8562 0381

Sicily travel guide 2023

Cuisines To Try On Your Visit To Sicily

The Strait of Messina divides Sicily from the Italian mainland and lies only 100 miles north of Tunisia. Sicily has a rich, intricate, and uniquely its own gastronomic culture. The island only joined Italy in 1860, giving distinctive, traditional dishes like arancini and cassata plenty of time to develop in a delectable culinary bubble.

The island's position on the Mediterranean, as well as its Greek, French, Spanish, and North African neighbors, had a significant influence on its cuisine. Many of Sicily's most well-known dishes use regional, sun-drenched ingredients like shellfish, olives, raisins, eggplant, capers, and tomatoes rather than the eggy kinds of pasta, cheese, and cured ham of the north. The area is well-known for its Italian confections, which include cannoli and granita. Ready to create your culinary tour? The best meals to sample if you want to experience Sicilian cuisine are listed below.

1. The Arancini

Arancini are said to have been inspired historically by rice meals made during the 9th and 11th centuries when the Arabs governed Sicily. The modern version of arancini is a breaded, deep-fried risotto ball that may be stuffed with just about anything, including tomato and mozzarella, ragu, and ham with béchamel, depending on the available fresh ingredients. Pick up a box of six from Da Cristina in Taormina and delight in the ideal snack while exploring the historic neighborhoods.

2. Pasta alla Norma

This well-known meal, made of sautéed eggplant, tomato sauce, fresh basil, and ricotta Salata, is perhaps a finer work of art than the opera by Sicilian Vincenzo Bellini from the 19th century that bears its name. One of the classic kinds of pasta in Italian cuisine, it's filling and herbaceous. The greatest may be found at La Pentolaccia Trattoria in Catania.

3. Cannoli

Unquestionably, cannoli, which are fried pastry tubes filled with fresh, creamy ricotta, is one of Sicily's most well-known exports. Every municipality has a special cannoli recipe that it considers to be the best. There are two that stand out: Dattilo's Euro Bar and More Bar's classic cannoli, which are made in Piana Degli Albanesi and are made on the sweeter side with extra sugar, candied fruit, and chocolate crumbs.

The pastries are stuffed to the brim with rich handmade ricotta after the cooks there make enormous, very crispy shells that are about the size of a sandwich plate.

4. Sfincione

You probably won't see this carb-filled delight until you smell it—the kind that's like a combination between focaccia and deep-dish pizza. Sfincione is a typical lunch or mid-morning snack in Palermo and the towns around. It is either served plain or topped with tomato sauce, onions, caciocavallo cheese, and anchovies. Try not to ruin your appetite for the rest of the day by purchasing one from a street seller or bakery.

5. Sardinian Pasta

Sicilian food is rich in seafood, possibly best known for its pasta con le sarde. It's a common meal on the Palermo side of the island, where residents and visitors alike congregate at La Cambusa to indulge in a hearty bowl of fresh fennel and oil-packed sardines over long pasta like bucatini or spaghetti. Golden raisins, pine nuts, and saffron serve as a reminder of the dish's North African heritage.

6. Sicilian Cassata

This exquisite dessert in the Baroque style may first seem to be Jell-o, but after just one mouthful, you'll be yearning for more. Ricotta cheese, marzipan-colored pistachio, white frosting, and candied fruit are piled over a sponge cake that has been soaked in liqueur for Easter. Even the Sicilians have a saying that goes, "Sad is the one who does not eat cassata on Easter morning." At bakeries like the 124-year-old Caffe Sicilia, tourists may, fortunately, sample cassata all year round.

7. The Caponata

The greatest food from the island, including celery, eggplant, tomatoes, and onion, is included in caponata, a dish that is enjoyed across the globe. The dish's specific ingredients might vary, but it often includes raisins, pine nuts, capers, olives, and sweetened vinegar. It is typically served at room temperature and has a great sweet-sour balance. At Trattoria U Fucularu in Catania, savor it as a component of the antipasto.

8. Serve With Trapanese Pesto.

The pesto trapanese is just as wonderful, even though pesto from northern Italy often receives all the attention. (The relationship is most likely explained by an ancient trading route between Genoa and Sicily.)

The Sicilian variety is composed of basil, garlic, tomatoes, almonds, and Pecorino cheese and is often served over busiate, a small pasta with a corkscrew form from Trapani. Al Vicoletto is at the top of the list of eateries in the town that serve the dish bearing its name.

9. Granita

Sicilian ice, also known as granita, is considerably simpler to get now than it was when it was first carried by day workers from the island's volcanic peaks. This tasty slushy delight may be had for breakfast with a brioche or coffee or as a refreshing afternoon treat since it is made with water, sugar, almonds, and fruit. (Speaking about a good day's start.) Almond, coffee, lemon, peach, and pistachio are among the tastes that are often offered by merchants like Catania's Pasticceria Savia.

10. Panelle

These chickpea flour fritters, which have a lot of similarities with other foods made with chickpeas like farinata and pakoras, were developed in Sicily under the Arab occupation, along with many other Silician delicacies. They are excellent when sandwiched between two slices of bread, however, they may be consumed alone. Grab one from a Palermo street seller and tuck it on while it's still hot.

CHAPTER 4

Practical Steps To Avoid Crowd When Touring In Sicily

Sicily is a renowned tourist destination known for its stunning beaches, historic sites, and mouthwatering cuisine. But in some of the island's busiest tourist areas during the busiest travel times, it may become extremely busy. Here are some suggestions to keep in mind if you want to visit Sicily without the crowds and have a great time:

The best time to visit Sicily is often from June to August, so schedule your vacation around this time. To escape the crowds and take advantage of the nicer weather, schedule your vacation outside of these months if you can. Because the weather is still pleasant and there are fewer people around, the shoulder seasons of spring and autumn are excellent choices.

Consider visiting less well-known locations: While Taormina and Palermo are well-liked tourist sites,

Sicily has numerous more locations that are as stunning and less crowded. Consider traveling to places like Agrigento, which is home to the Valley of the Temples, a collection of ancient Greek ruins, or Noto, a Baroque town.

When visiting a major tourist destination during high season, try to avoid going at the busiest times. For instance, if you want to escape the crowds while visiting Syracuse, go there early in the morning or late in the day.

Consider going on a tour: If you're limited on time, think about going on a Sicily trip. A few tour operators provide small-group excursions that take you to less popular locations and keep you away from the throng.

Use public transportation to your advantage: Sicily boasts a sophisticated public transit system that may help you escape the crowds. Reach the less popular cities and villages via bus or rail.

Consider staying at a bed & breakfast or apartment locally instead of booking a room at a hotel in a busy tourist region. You will be able to dodge the crowds and explore the island like a native by doing this.

Have a backup plan in case a popular location proves to be busier than you anticipated. Plan B in mind, and be flexible with your schedule so you can adjust your plans right away if required.

Keep in mind that you are a visitor at someone else's house even if you are traveling to Sicily as a tourist. Avoid being boisterous and disruptive to show respect for the community and its culture.

These pointers will help you travel in Sicily in a way that is more tranquil and genuine. You may take your time to soak in the island's splendor and uncover secret attractions that the majority of visitors never see. Keep in mind that you can always ask locals for suggestions and advice on how to escape the crowds; they will be eager to assist.

1-Week itinerary

It might be difficult to create the ideal itinerary with so much to see and do. A proposed one-week schedule is provided below to assist you in exploring all of Sicily and having a great trip:

Day 1: Arrive in Palermo

Take a taxi from Palermo Airport to your hotel in the heart of the city. See the magnificent Palermo Cathedral, the Teatro Massimo, and the vibrant Ballar Market while spending the day touring the city's ancient district. Dinner at one of the city's top restaurants is a great way to round off the day.

Day 2: Explore Palermo and Monreale

See the magnificent Monreale Church to begin the day, which is well-known for its magnificent mosaics. See the Palace dei Normanni, a former royal residence that today houses the Sicilian Regional Assembly, after which you return to Palermo. Visit the Palermo Capuchin Catacombs in the afternoon to observe the thousands of mummified bodies on display there.

Day 3: Visit Agrigento and the Valley of the Temples

Take the train to Agrigento, a UNESCO World Heritage site well-known for its ancient Greek ruins, in the morning. The Valley of the Temples is a spectacular collection of temples and historical buildings that provide an insight into ancient Greek culture and architecture. Spend the day exploring it.

Day 4: Enjoy the Beaches of Taormina

Catch the early-morning train to Taormina, a lovely town on Sicily's east coast. Spend the day relaxing on the lovely beaches, discovering the town's historic district, and admiring the breathtaking Mount Etna vistas.

Day 5: Explore Mount Etna

The tallest active volcano in Europe, Mount Etna, may be explored on a guided tour. Visit the Silvestri Craters, take a beautiful stroll through the lava fields, and discover the geology and history of the volcano. Return to Taormina in the evening for dinner and cocktails.

Day 6: Discover Syracuse and Ortigia Island

The morning train will take you to Syracuse, a stunning seaside city with a fascinating history. See the Greek remains in the Neapolis Archaeological Park before traveling to the little island of Ortigia to discover its winding alleyways, historical structures, and breathtaking waterfront.

Day 7: Relax in Cefalù

Get on the train in the morning and travel to Cefalù, a picturesque coastal town renowned for its magnificent beaches, quaint medieval alleyways, and stunning cathedral. Enjoy a day of beach relaxation, town exploration, and mouthwatering regional cuisine. Enjoy a breathtaking sunset view from the town's promenade to cap off the day.

Day 8: Departure from Palermo

Return to Palermo by rail in the morning to catch your flight home. Spend some time in the city, if you have the time, before you go.

With this plan, you can experience the finest of Sicily in only one week, including the Agrigento ancient ruins, Taormina's breathtaking beaches, and Syracuse's lovely city. You'll enjoy an incredible trip that highlights the best of Sicily's history, culture, and natural beauty if you stick to this plan.

Festivals You Are Likely To Celebrate On Your Vacation In Sicily

Sicily is an attractive island in southern Italy with a diverse culture. It is renowned for its gorgeous beaches, mouthwatering cuisine, and energetic festivals. On your trip to Sicily, you may choose to see any of the following festivals:

One of the most significant holidays in Sicily is La Festa di San Giuseppe (St. Joseph's Day), which is observed on March 19. The island's patron saint, St. Joseph, is honored at this religious feast. In addition to the creation of specific meals like "sfinge" (a sort of fried bread) and "zeppole," the celebration is distinguished by vibrant parades, traditional music, and dance (sweet fried dough).

Santa Rosalia, the patron saint of Palermo, is honored during this event called La Fiera di Santa Rosalia. Parades, live music, and fireworks are all part of the week-long celebration that takes place every July. The procession of the Santa Rosalia statue through Palermo's streets as it is accompanied by traditional music and dance is the festival's high point.

La Fiera della Madonna della Lettera is a celebration in Caltagirone, Italy, in honor of the Virgin Mary. It takes place in August and includes a Madonna della Lettera statue procession through the town's streets. The event is accompanied by traditional music and dance, and thousands of vibrant ceramic tiles are used to embellish the monument.

In May and June, all of Sicily participates in La Festa dei Crocifissi. It is a religious holiday honoring the cross, and it is observed with vibrant parades, ethnic music and dance, and the cooking of unique cuisine.

In Piana Degli Albanesi, a festival called La Fiera di San Matteo is held in St. Matthew's honor. The statue of St. Matthew is carried through the town's streets during the procession, which happens every September. A wonderful chance to learn about the distinctive culture and customs of the Albanian population in Sicily is provided by the festival, which is accompanied by traditional music and dance.

La Fiera di San Giovanni is a celebration in Randazzo, Italy, in honor of St. John the Baptist. A procession of the St. John statue through the town's streets is a hallmark of the June celebration. The festival, which features traditional music and dance, is a wonderful chance to learn about the town's distinctive culture and customs.

These are but a handful of the many festivals that are held throughout the year in Sicily. The chance to explore the island's vibrant culture and customs is provided by each one individually. There is likely to be a festival that piques your interest, whether it has excellent food, religious events, or traditional music and dance.

CONCLUSION

Sicily is a beautiful island with lots to offer everyone. Sicily is a place that everyone should travel to at least once in their lifetime because of its fascinating history, vibrant culture, gorgeous beaches, and breathtaking scenery. The goal of this travel handbook was to highlight the best of Sicily, including the vibrant metropolis of Palermo, the historic ruins of Agrigento, and the stunning beaches of Taormina.

We hope that this travel guide has given you all the information you need to plan an enjoyable trip to Sicily. Sicily has much to offer everyone, whether they are history buffs, foodies, or just looking for some adventure and relaxation. We invite you to discover the island's many undiscovered attractions, which range from quaint towns to undiscovered beaches.

We advise you to immerse yourself in the community's culture, sample the delectable cuisine, and get to know the welcoming inhabitants as you begin your Sicilian trip. We wish you a journey to

Sicily that is full of lifelong memories and wonderful experiences.

Printed in Great Britain
by Amazon